MW01297164

ColoringBook

By Banana leaves

....

Colorist's Name

....

Date

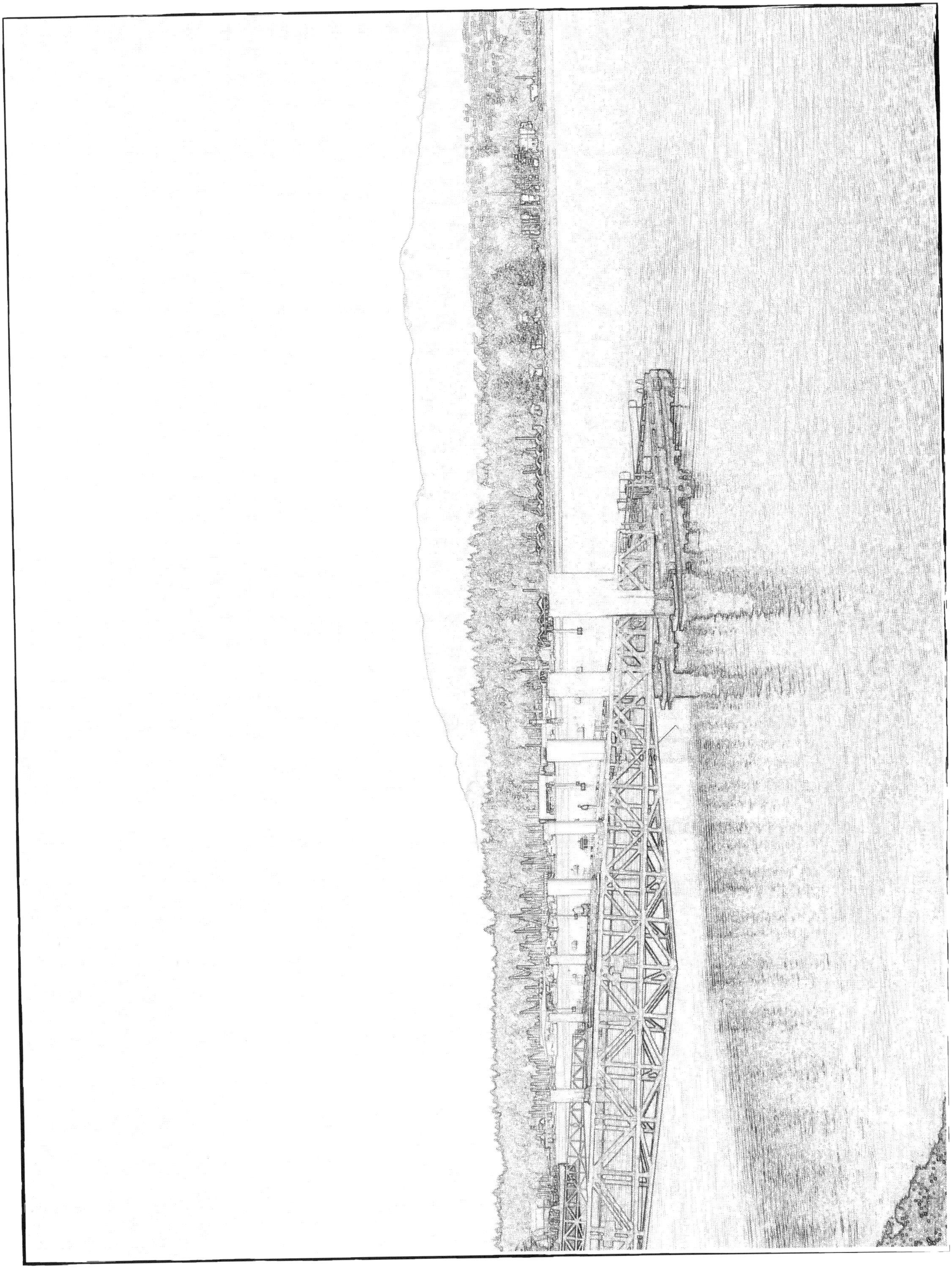

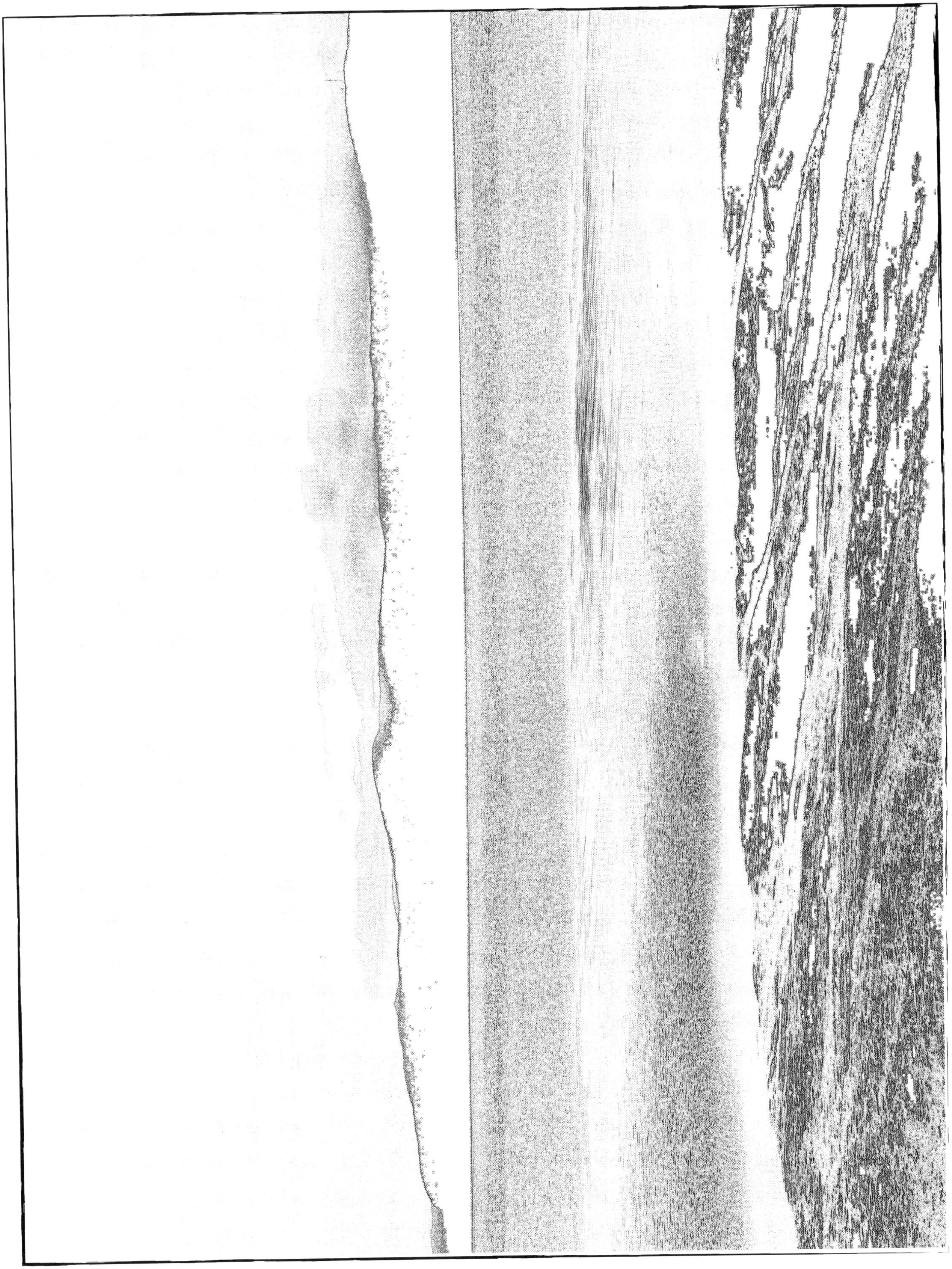

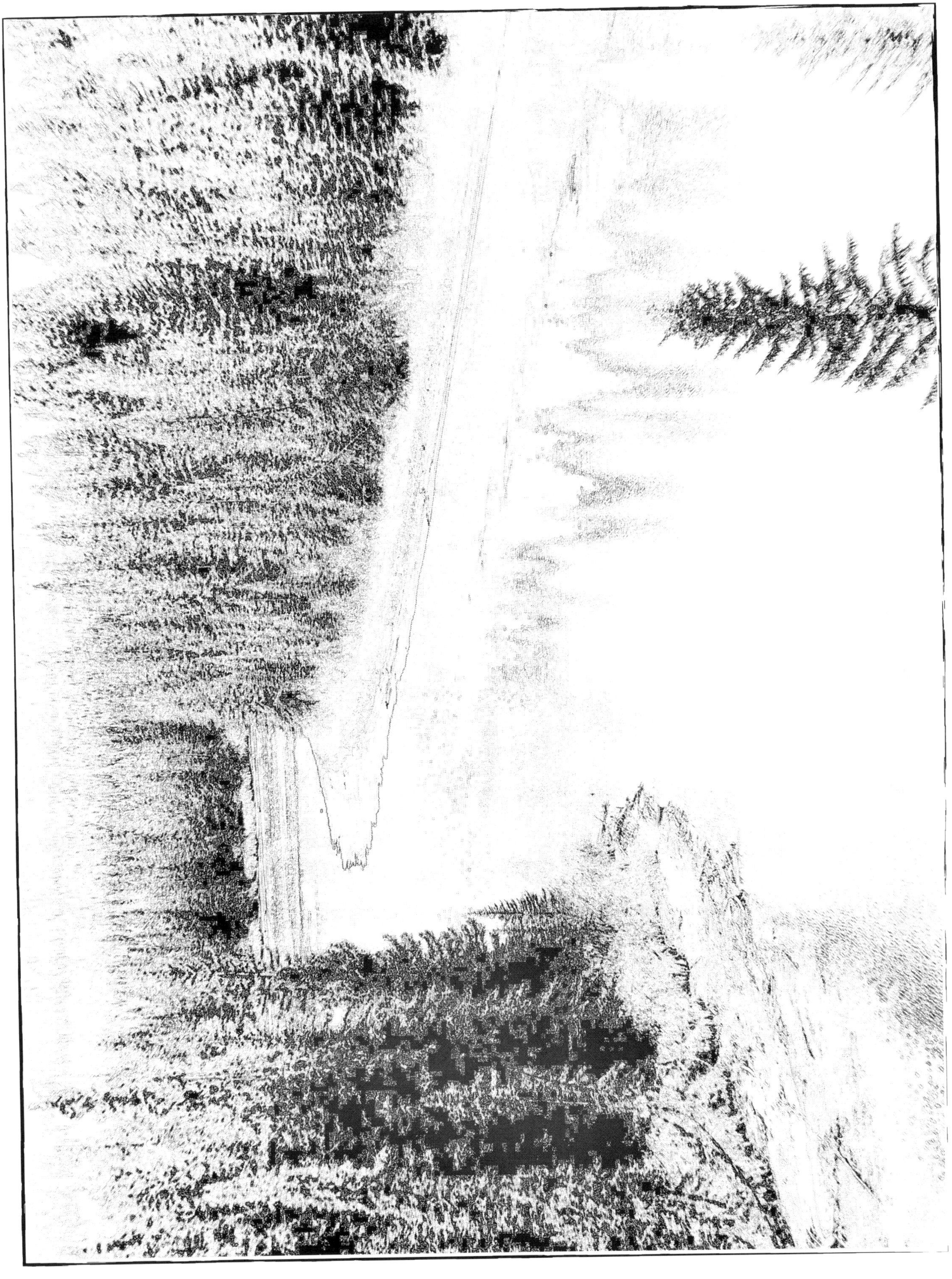

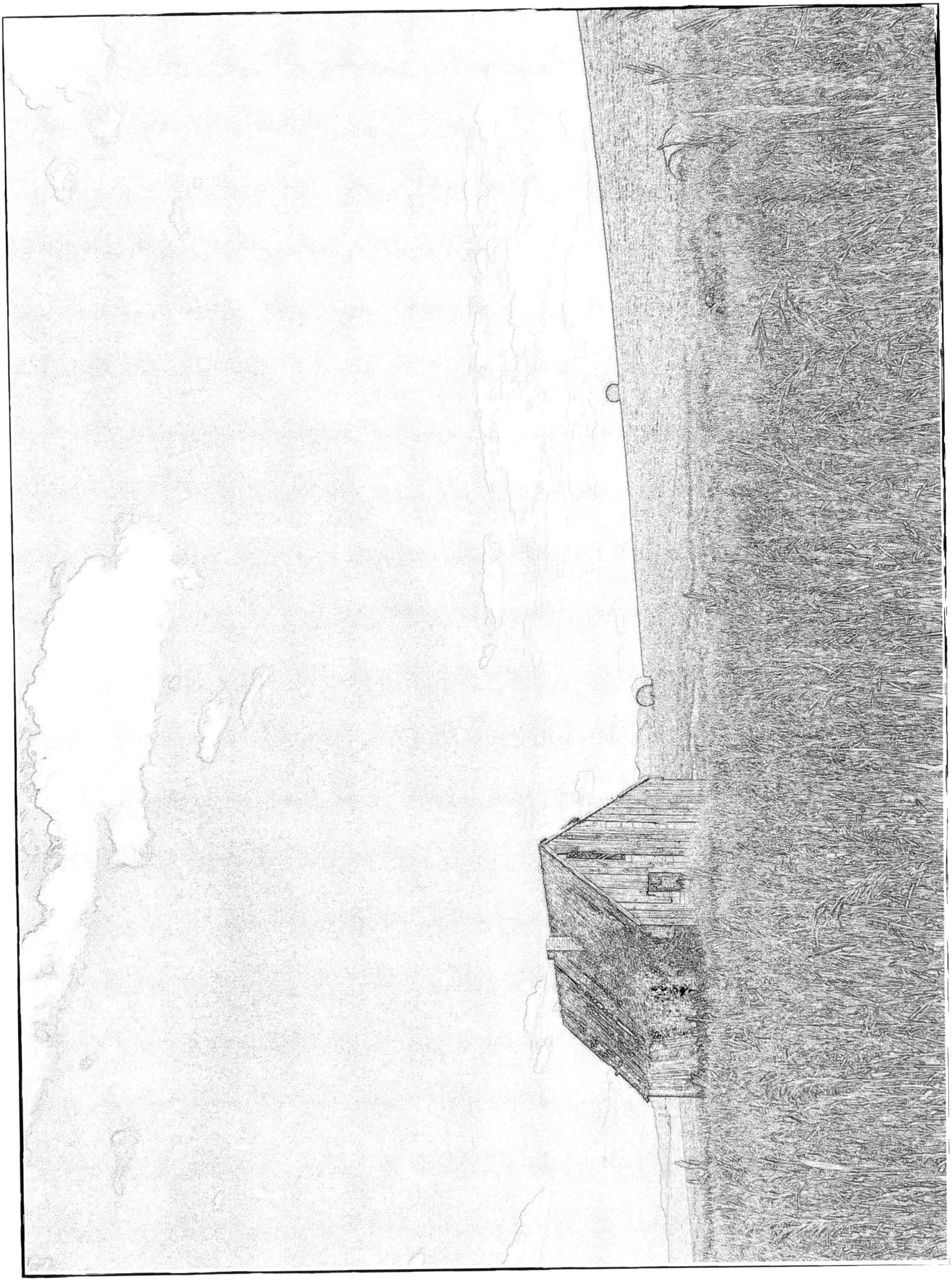

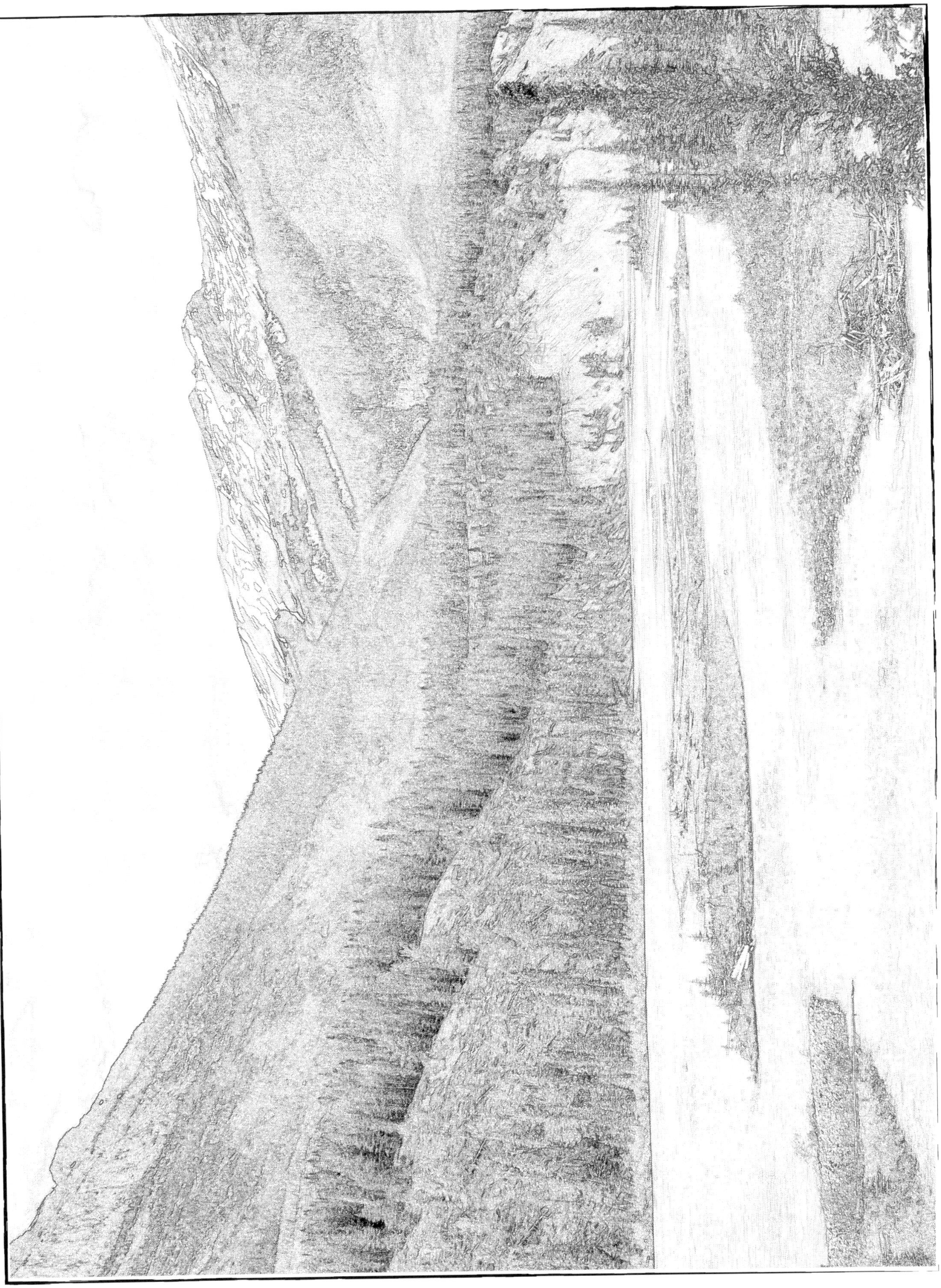

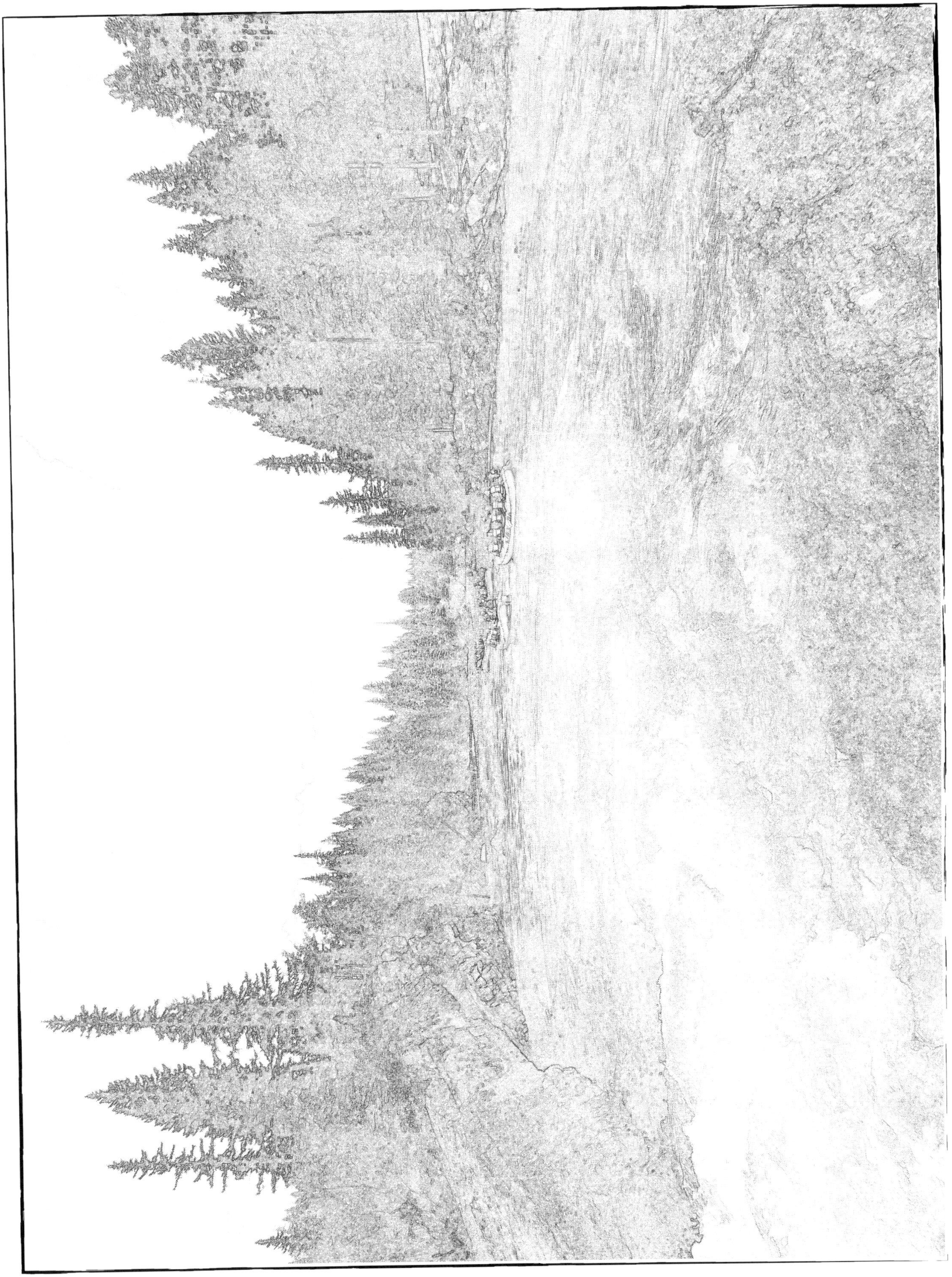

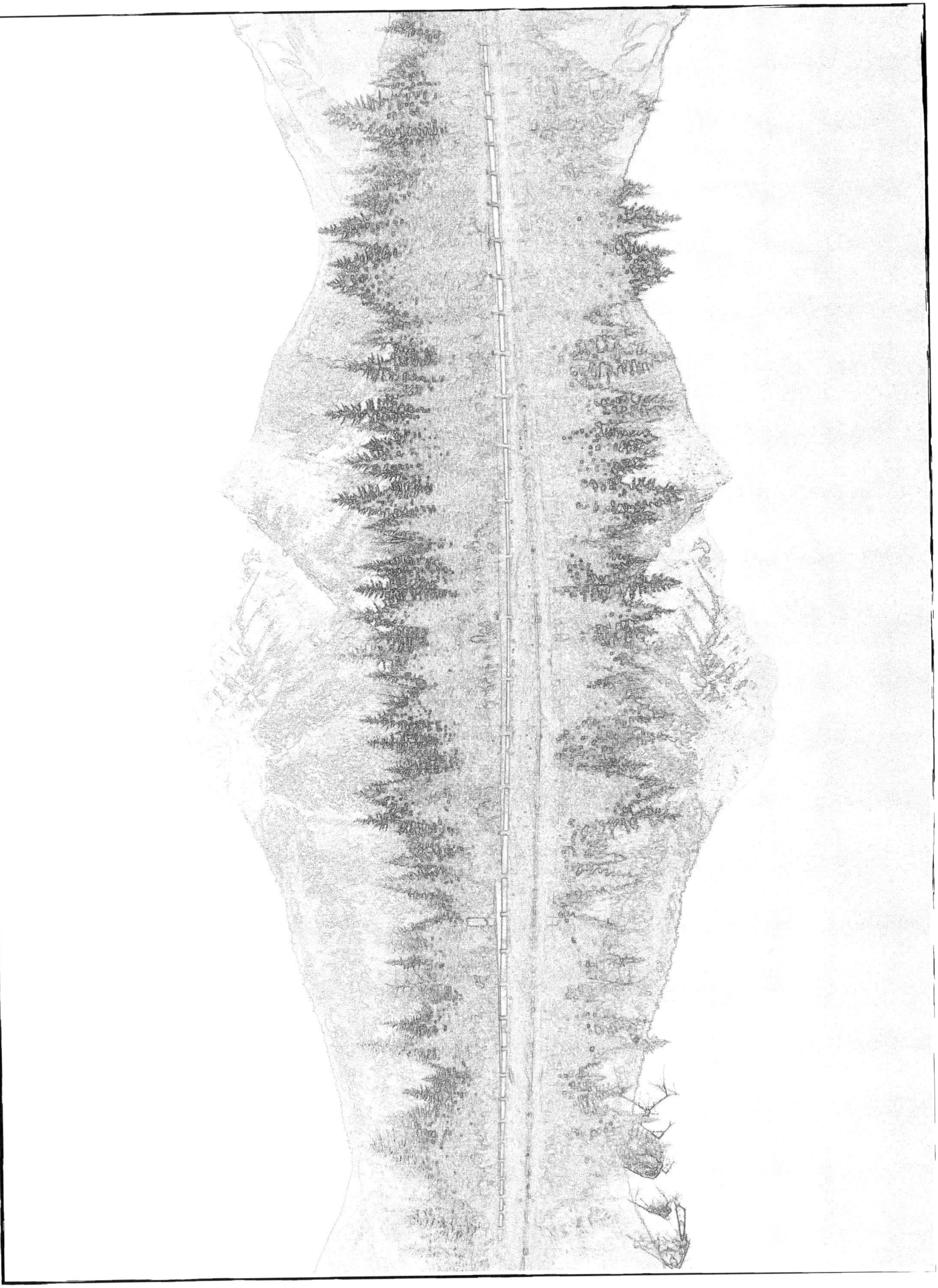

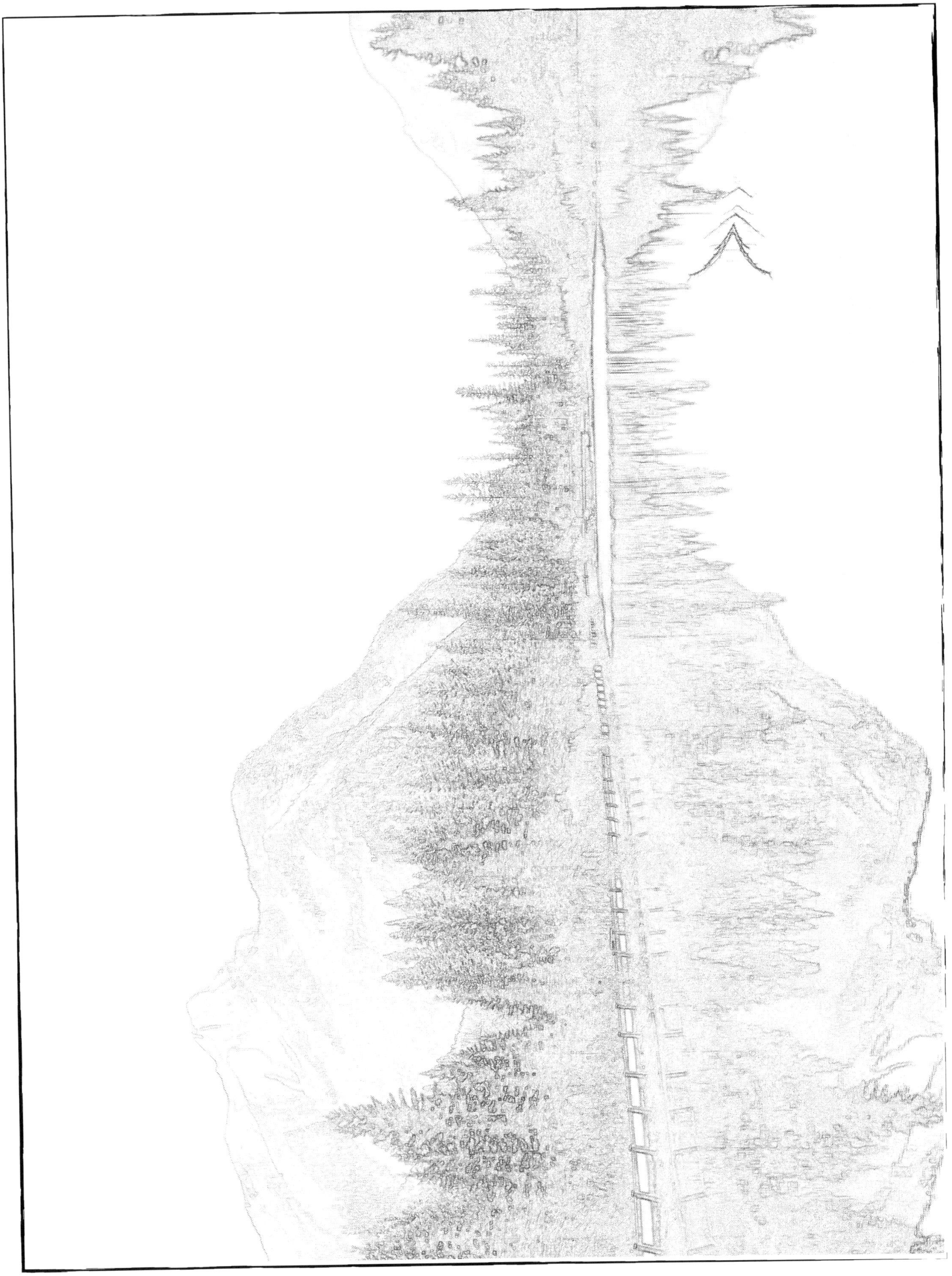

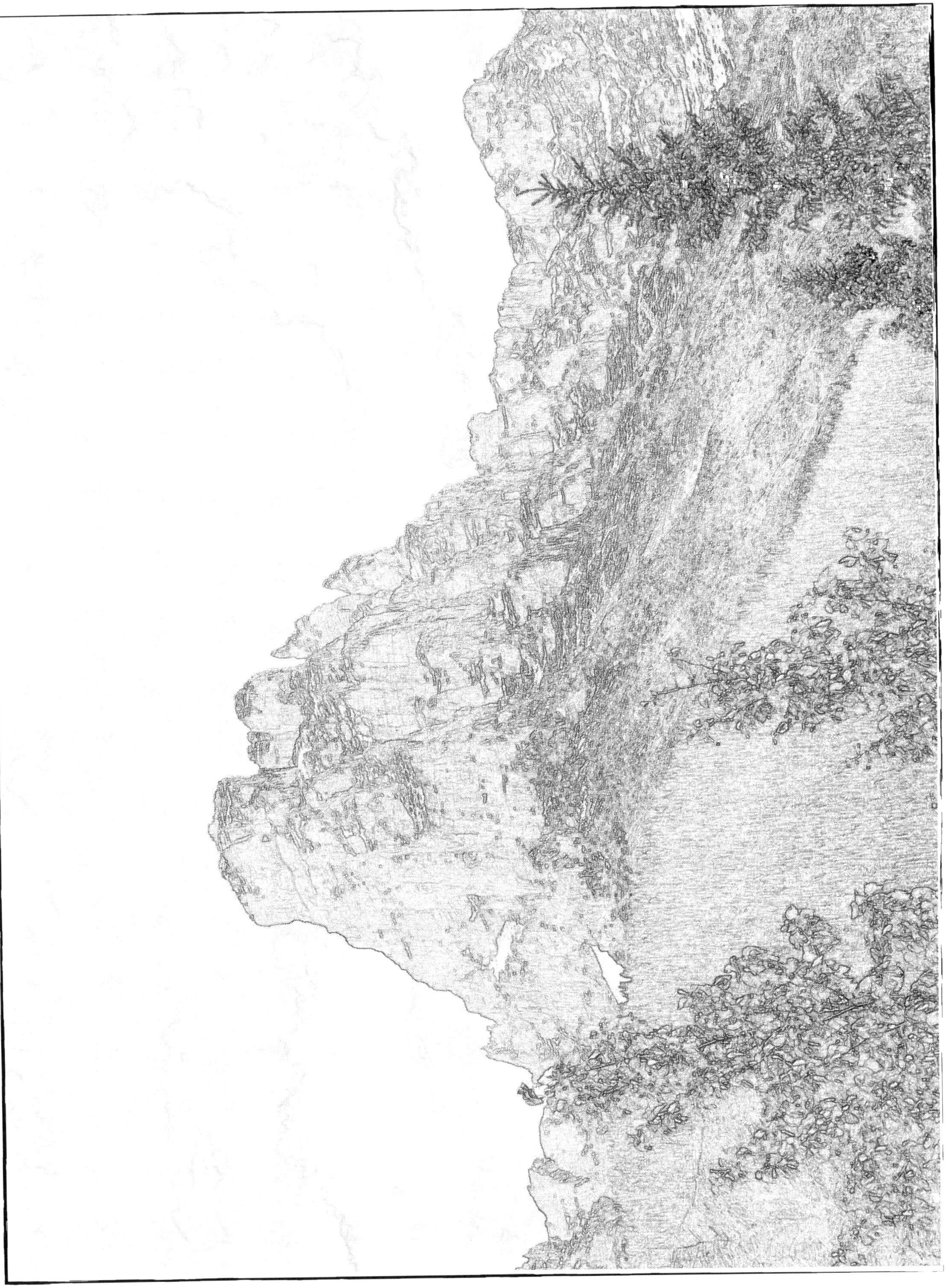

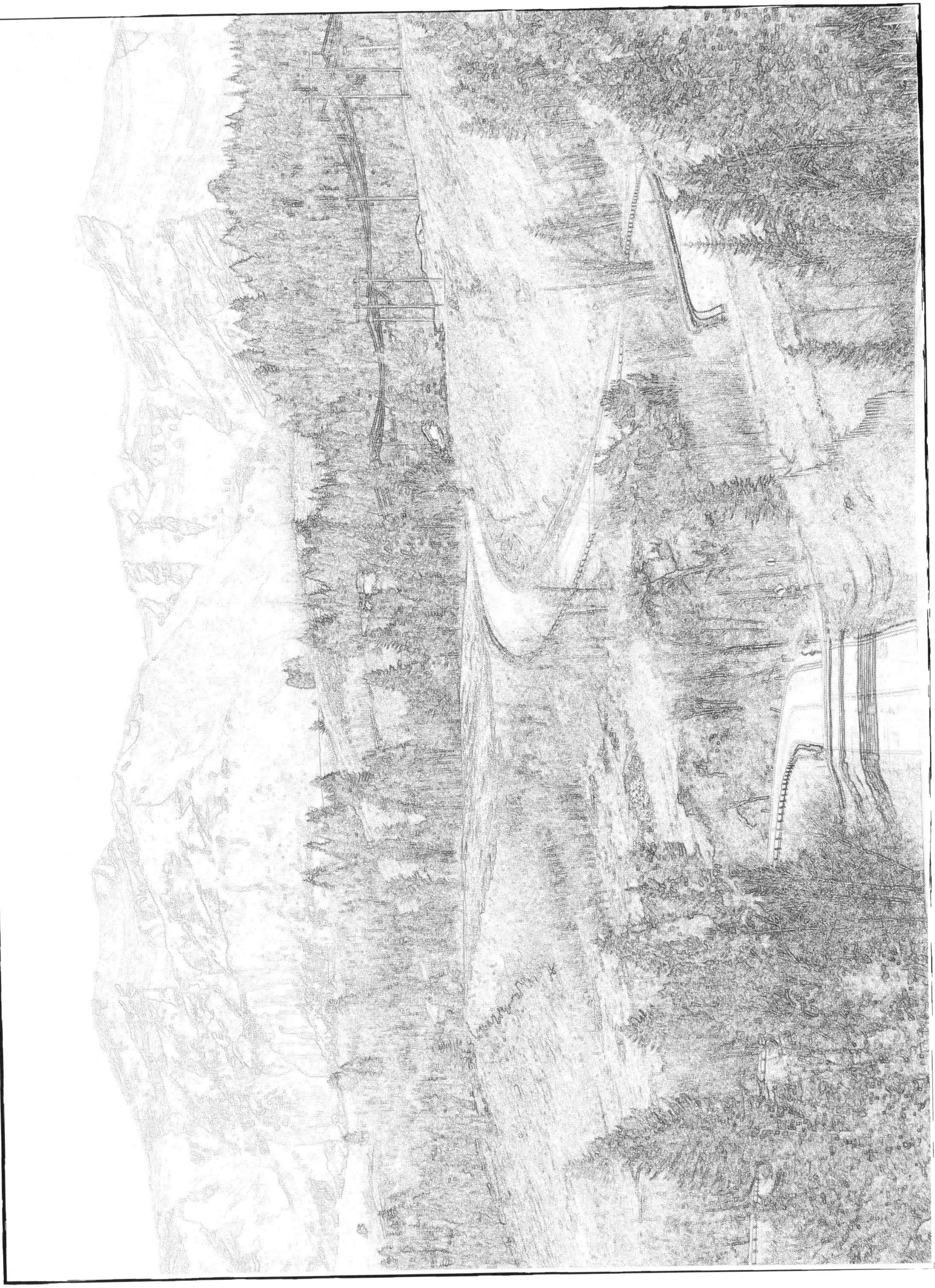

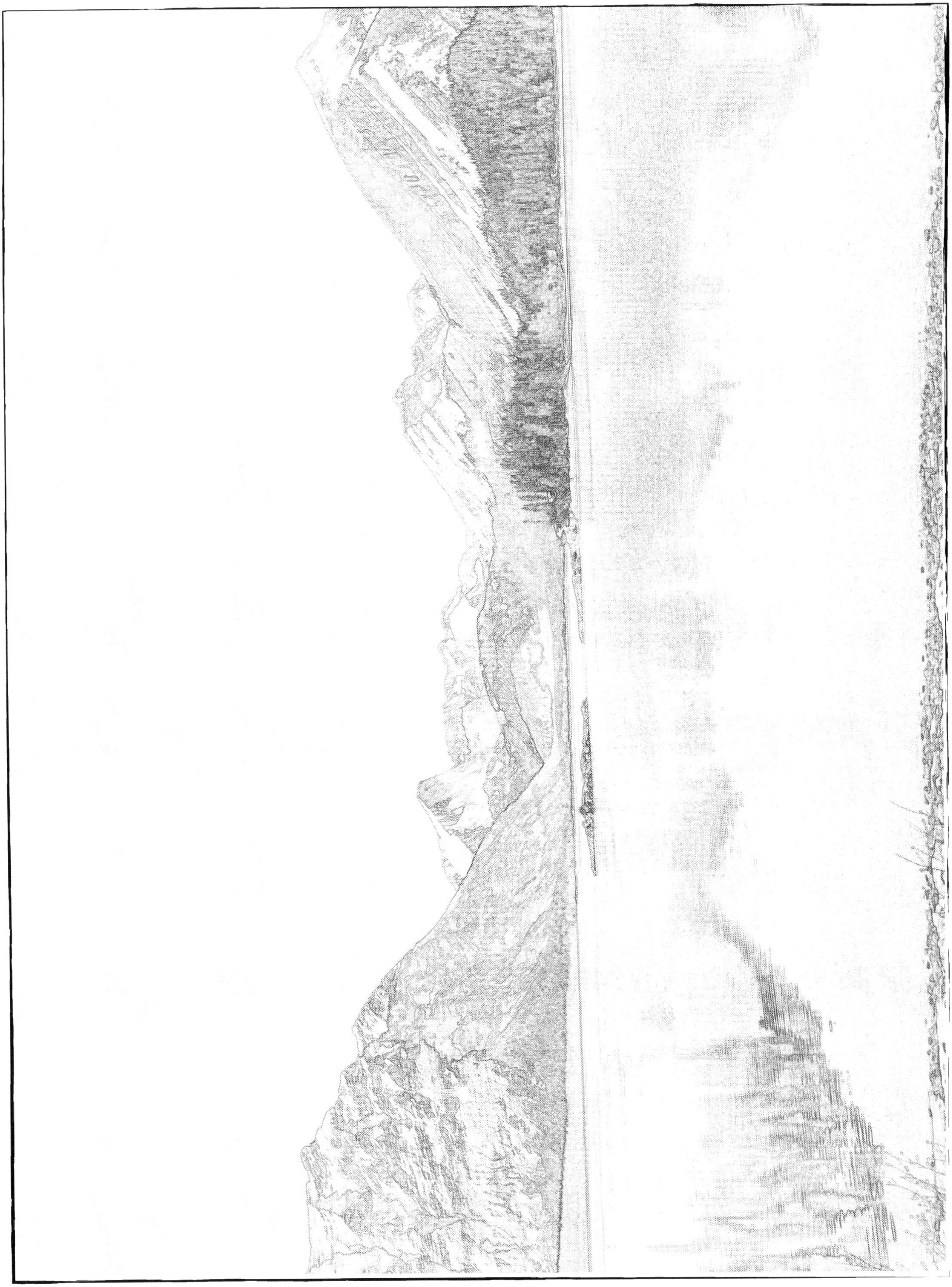

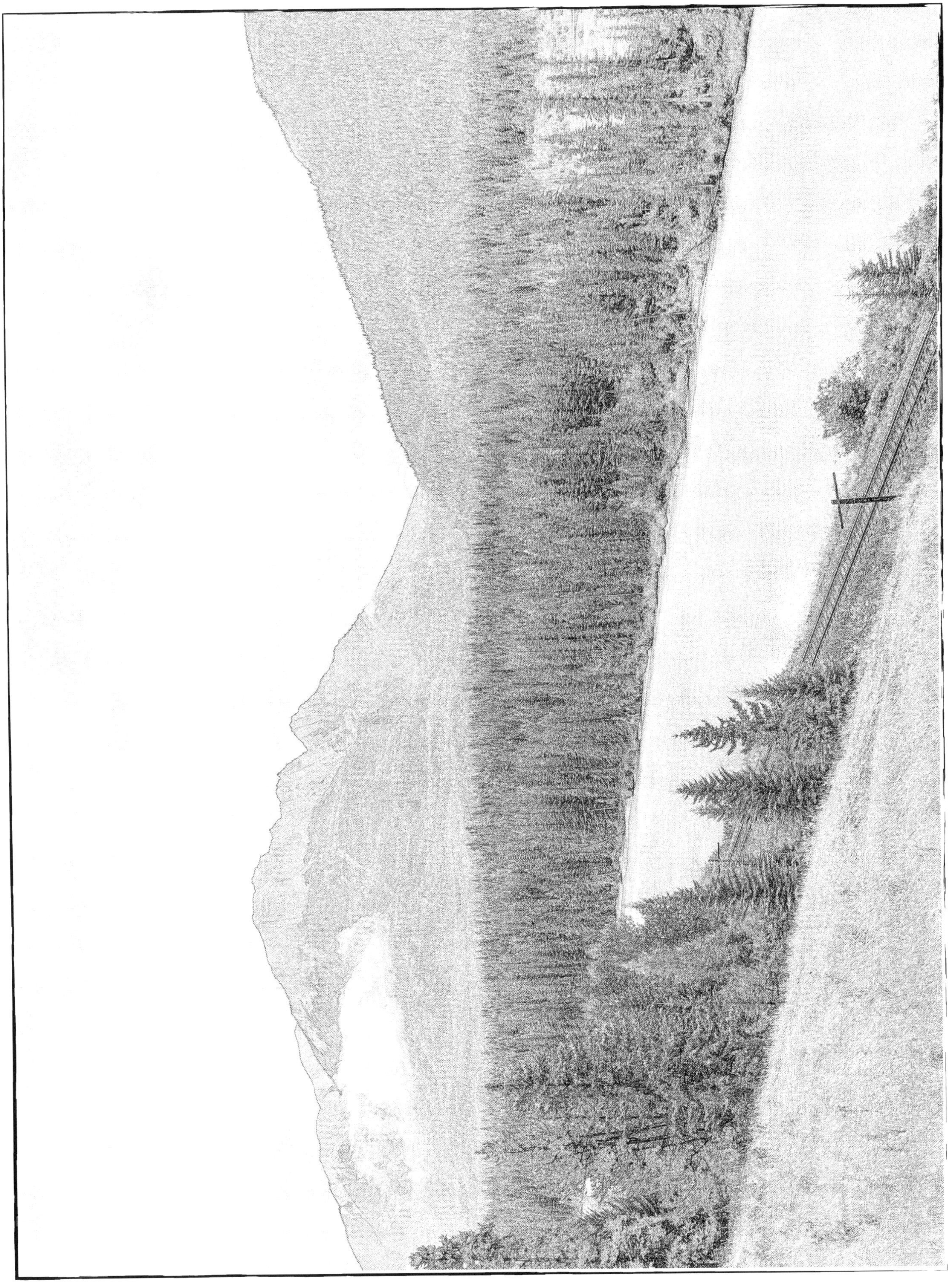

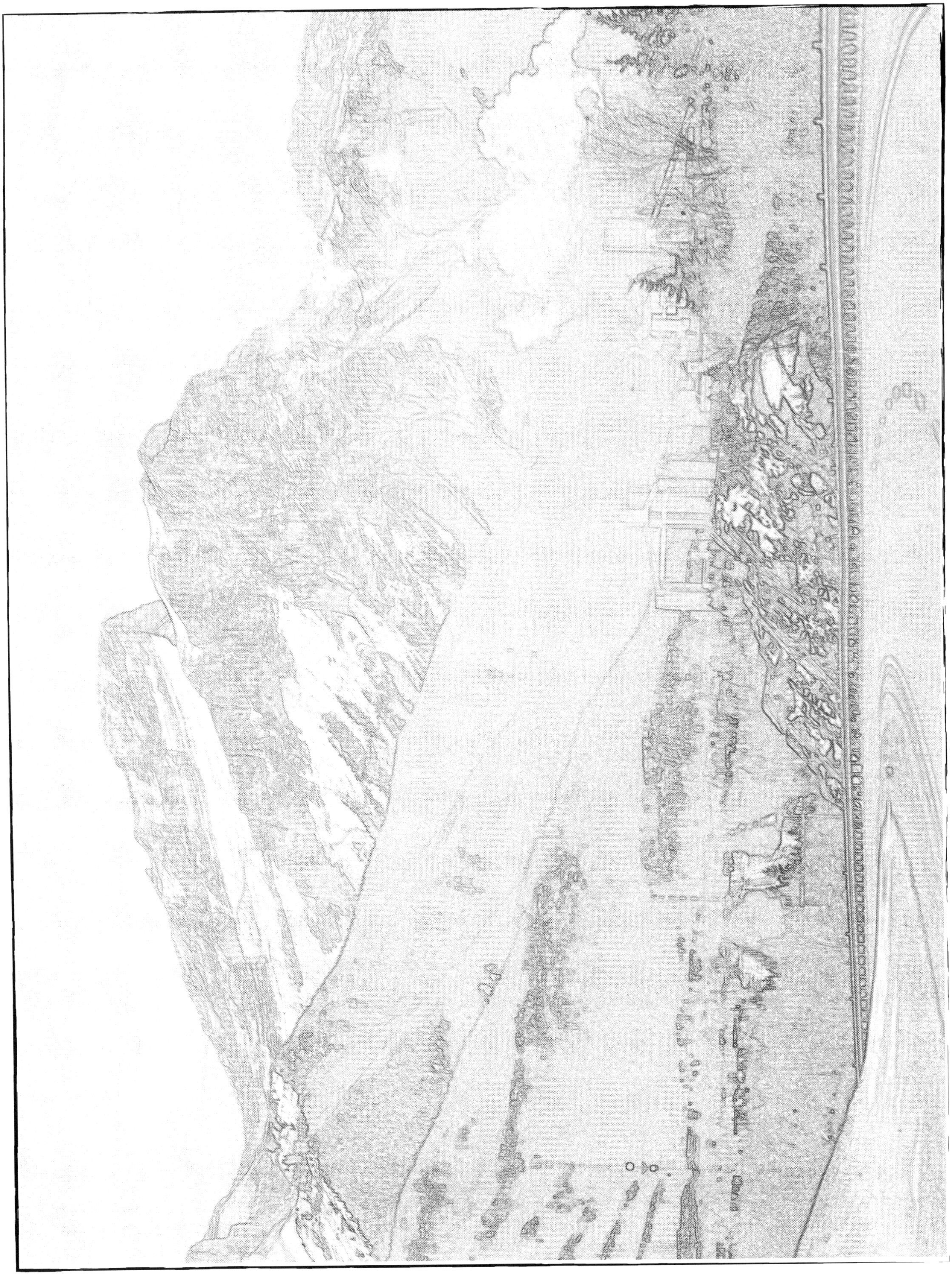

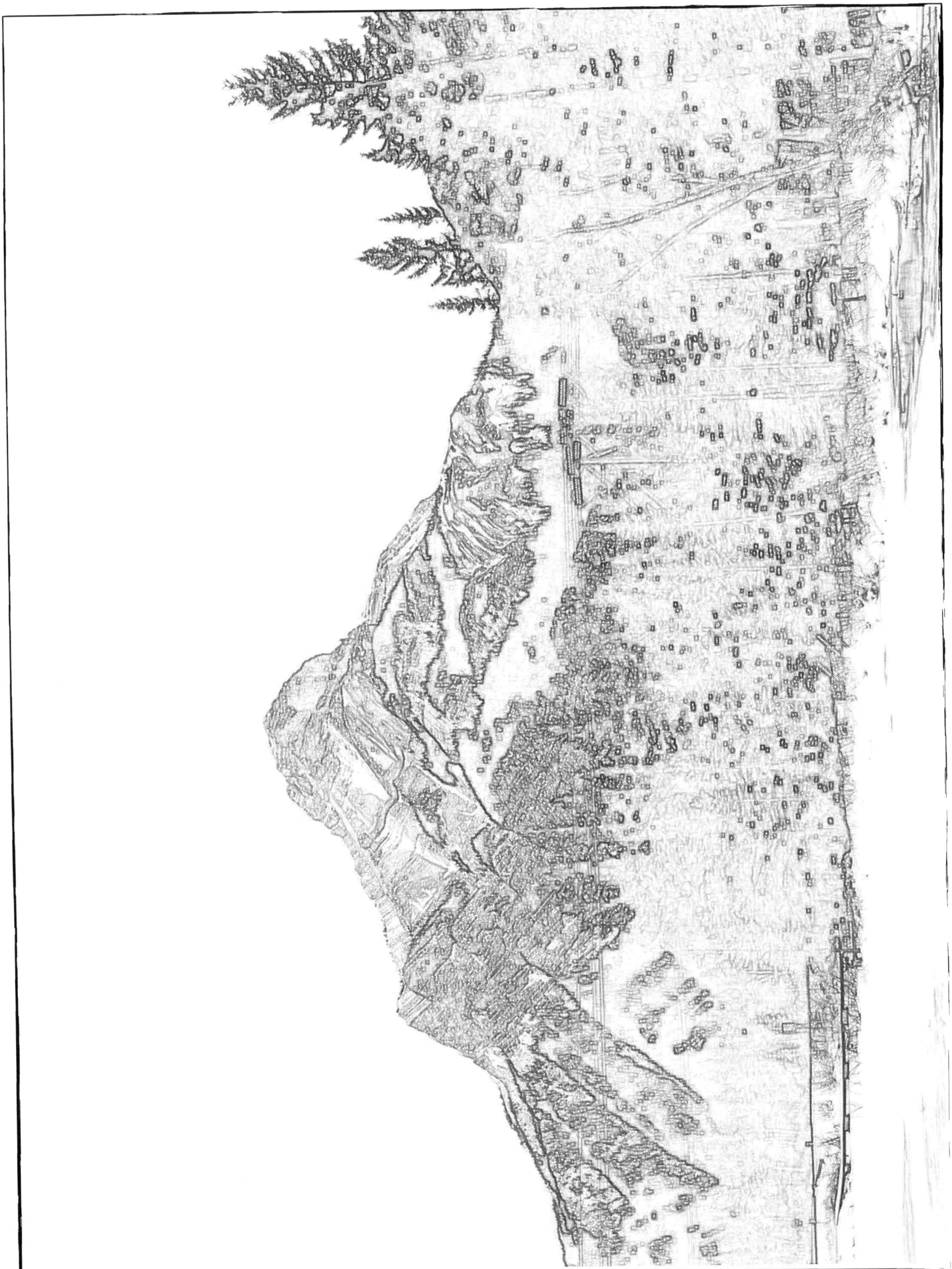

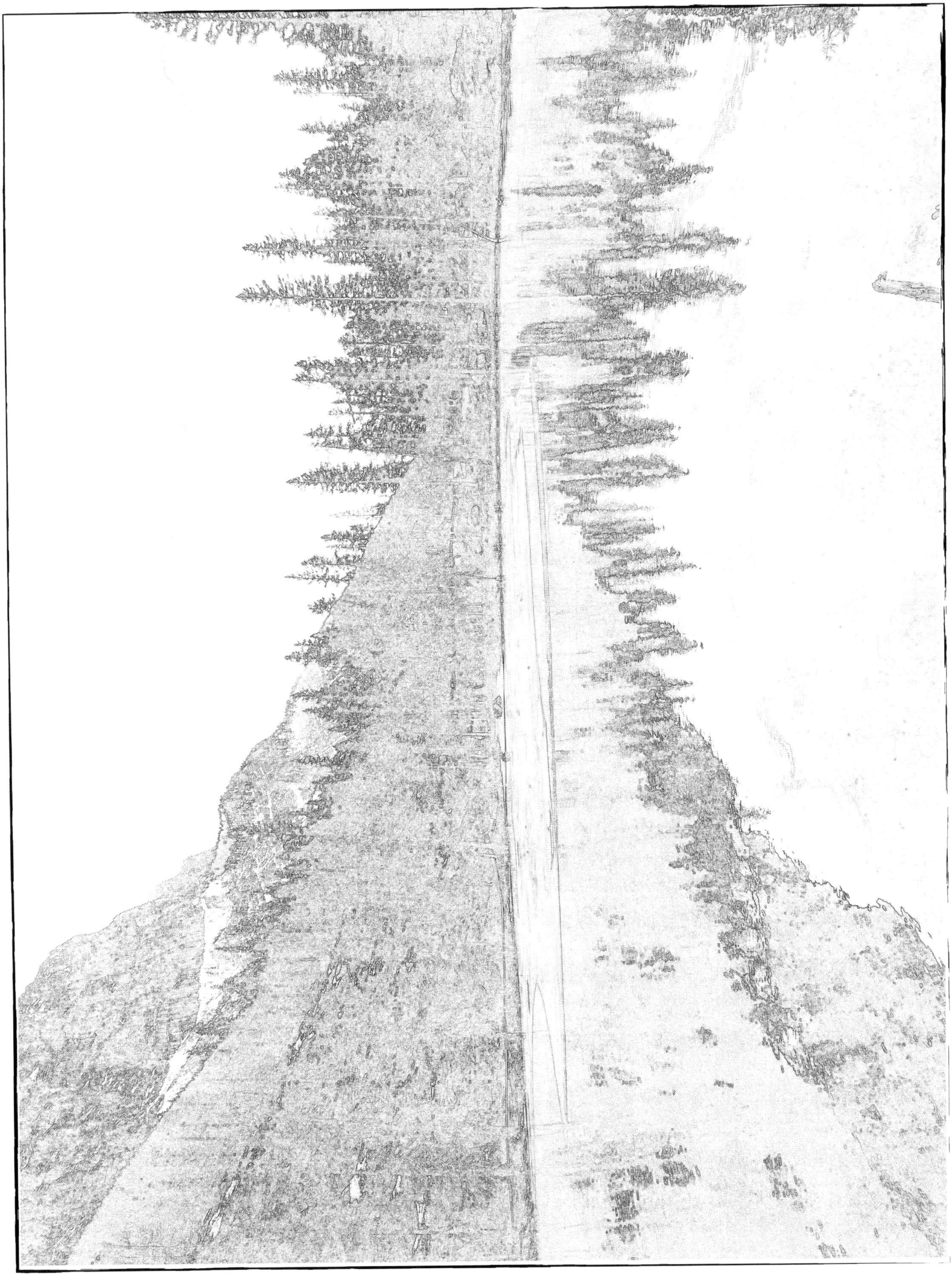

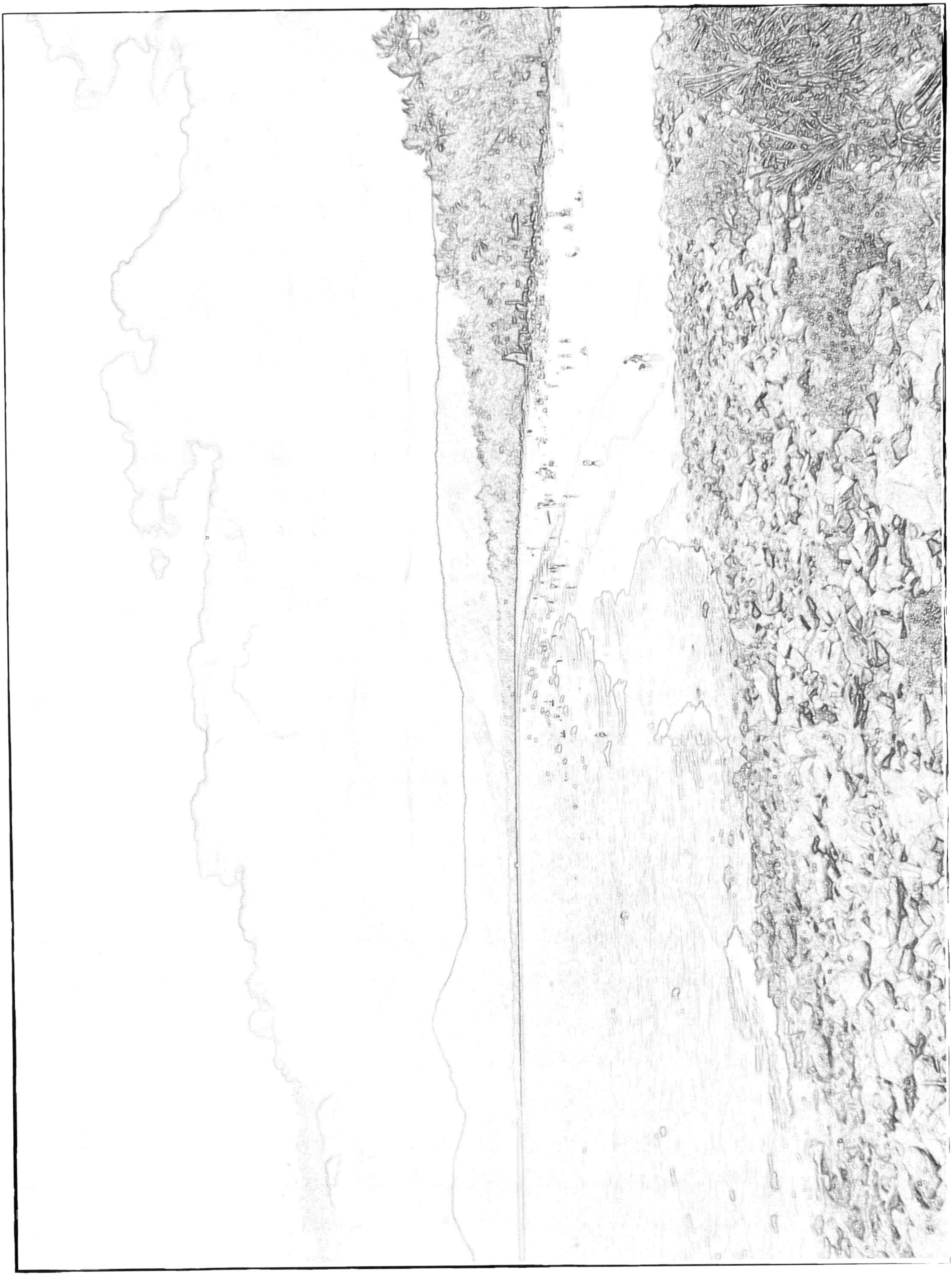

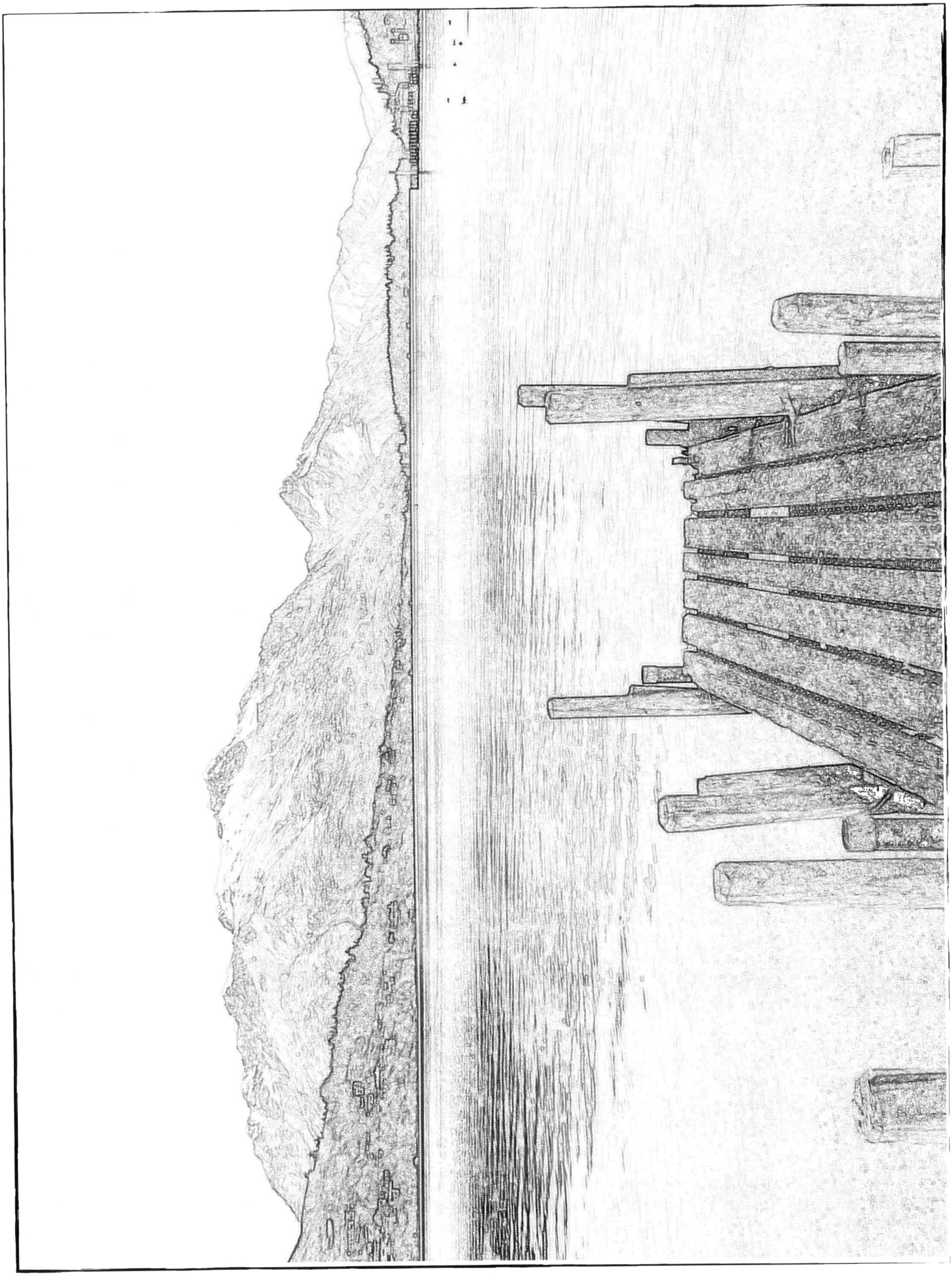

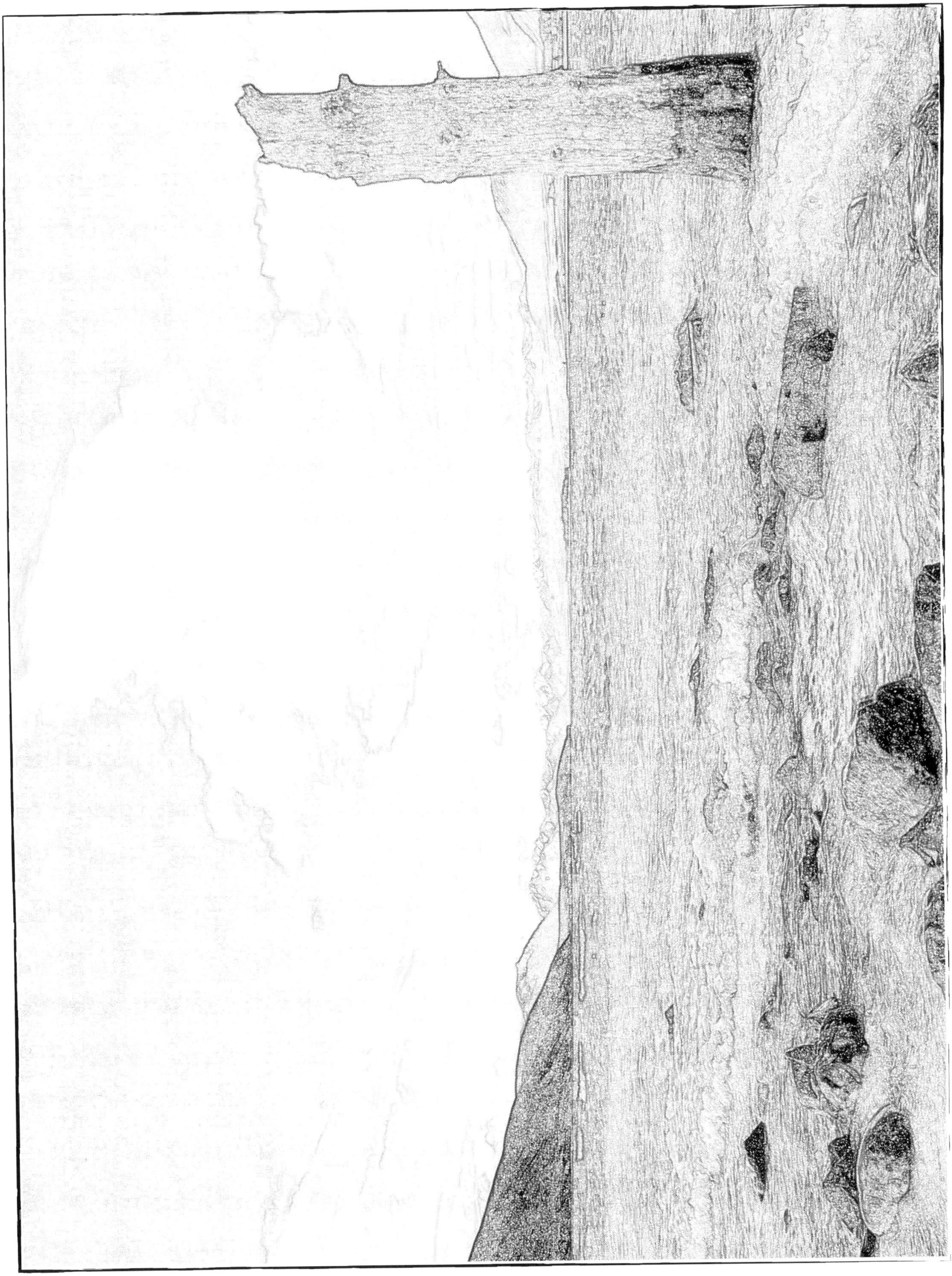

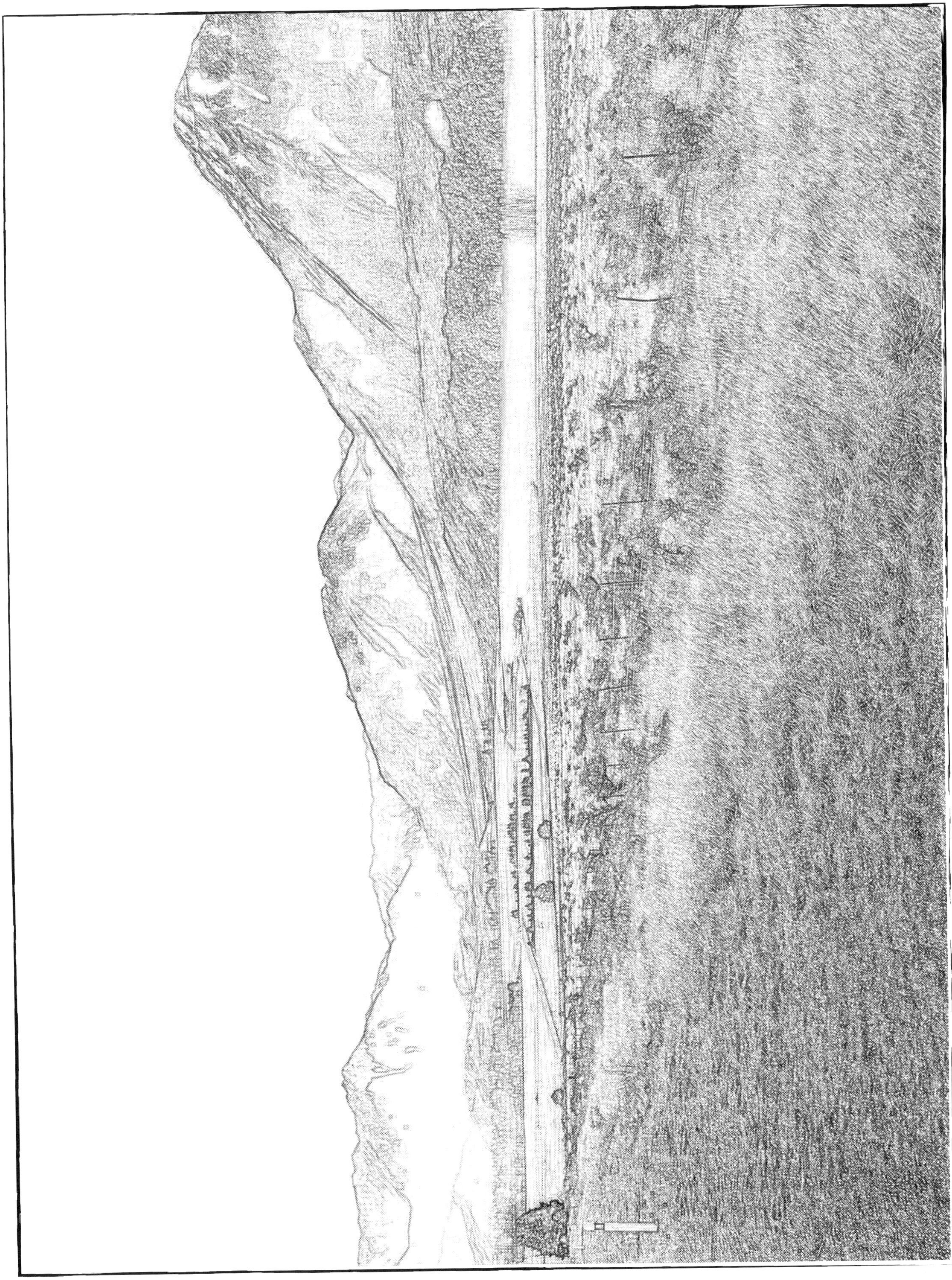

65580773R00036

Made in the USA
Lexington, KY
17 July 2017